Stop Yourself From Overthinking

Practical Steps To Break Free From Too Much Rumination

By

Adam Vaney

Table of Contents

Introduction

Here was Henry, a traveler standing at a crossroads, weighed down by the burden of indecision. Each path offers its own promises and perils, yet he finds themselves paralyzed by overthinking. He has analyzed every possible outcome, yet he's trapped in a maze of doubt and uncertainty.

As the hours pass, the sun sets low on the horizon, casting long shadows across the crossroads. Henry remains rooted in place, haunted by the relentless chatter of their mind. He envisions scenarios of success and failure, happiness and regret until the lines between reality and imagination blur.

Amid his mental turmoil, a wise elder, Omar approaches, his face weathered with age yet radiating tranquility. With a gentle smile, Omar offers a simple yet profound question:

"What if you embraced the natural course of life instead of attempting to manipulate every result?"

Henry is struck by the wisdom of these words, realizing that his overthinking has only led to more confusion and distress. With a newfound sense of clarity, he takes a deep breath and releases the tight grip of his mind.

Embracing the uncertainty of the unknown, he chooses a path and sets forth with renewed determination. Though the journey ahead may be fraught with challenges, he trusts in his ability to navigate the twists and turns with grace and resilience.

The story above paints a vivid picture of a common struggle: the paralyzing effects of overthinking. Henry's story serves as a relatable example that many of us can identify with when faced with decision-making. If you've ever found yourself grappling with similar symptoms of overthinking, then this book is tailored to provide you with effective strategies to overcome this mental hurdle.

Understanding the Scope and Impact of the Overthinking Epidemic

Do you ever feel trapped in a relentless cycle of worry? Does your mind replay past conversations, catastrophize about future possibilities, and dissect every decision until it loses all meaning? If so, you're not alone. Welcome to the ever-growing club of overthinkers, where intrusive thoughts become unwelcome guests, permanently camped out in the penthouse suite of our mental landscape.

Overthinking isn't just a personal quirk; it's a widespread phenomenon reaching epidemic proportions. Studies suggest that nearly 80% of adults report engaging in regular overthinking, with women and high-achievers disproportionately affected.

This silent epidemic casts a long shadow and impacts every area of our life.

Mental well-being: Constant rumination fuels anxiety, depression, and low self-esteem, eroding our sense of peace and joy.

Physical health: Overthinking triggers the stress response, leading to headaches, sleep disturbances, and even weakened immunity.

Relationships: When our minds are preoccupied with worry, we struggle to be fully present and engaged with others, impacting our connections.

Productivity: Rumination paralyzes action, hinders decision-making, and steals precious time that could be spent on creative pursuits or meaningful activities.

But why are we collectively drowning in a sea of overthinking? The solution can be found in an intricate interaction of various elements.

- In a world once riddled with threats, our ancestors who over thought might have had a survival advantage. However, in today's safer environment, this tendency can backfire.
- The cult of perfectionism, the constant comparison game fueled by social media, and the fear of failure create a fertile ground for anxious overthinking.
- Our brains are wired to prioritize negative information, making us more likely to dwell on worst-case scenarios and past mistakes.
- Neuroticism, a tendency towards negative emotions, and high agreeableness predisposing one to please others, are linked to higher levels of overthinking.

Understanding the scope and impact of overthinking is the first step towards reclaiming control. By acknowledging the prevalence of this struggle and its far-reaching consequences, we can shed the shame and embark on a journey towards a more mindful and peaceful existence.

In the coming chapters, we'll delve deeper into the science of overthinking, unpack its roots, and equip you with powerful tools and techniques to break free from its grip. Remember, you are not defined by your thoughts, and you have the power to create a life free from the tyranny of overthinking.

Exploring the Science of Overthinking

Have you ever wondered why your mind loves to linger on negative thoughts, replay past scenarios, and rehearse worst-case futures? It's not just you. While overthinking might feel like a personal torment, science reveals a fascinating interplay between evolution, psychology, and the very architecture of our brains. Let's peek under the hood and explore why your brain gets stuck in overdrive, churning out a constant stream of overthinking:

1. Evolutionary Hangover: Imagine our ancestors navigating a world teeming with predators, uncertainties, and dangers. In such an environment, constantly analyzing potential threats and ruminating on past encounters might have held a survival advantage. This "worry wart" tendency, once adaptive, now manifests as overthinking in our relatively safer world, leading to unnecessary stress and anxiety.
2. The Negativity Bias: Our brains are wired to prioritize negative information. This negativity bias, likely stemming from the evolutionary need to avoid threats, makes

us more attuned to potential dangers and failures. Unfortunately, it also means our brains readily latch onto negative thoughts, amplifying them and fueling overthinking spirals.

3. The Amygdala's Alarm System: Deep within the brain lies the amygdala, our emotional alarm system. When triggered by perceived threats, real or imagined, the amygdala floods our body with stress hormones like cortisol, putting us on high alert. This "fight-or-flight" response, designed for acute danger, becomes dysregulated in chronic overthinkers, keeping the amygdala constantly on edge.

4. The Prefrontal Cortex's Overload: The prefrontal cortex, responsible for complex thought and decision-making, often gets hijacked by overthinking. Instead of focusing on the present moment or problem-solving, it gets entangled in repetitive worry loops, unable to disengage from the mental chatter.

5. The Dopamine Connection: Remember the satisfying feeling of finally figuring something out? That's dopamine, a reward neurotransmitter released by the brain when we learn or solve problems. Ironically, overthinking can mimic this reward system, creating a false sense of progress through rumination, even though it offers no real solutions.

6. The Power of Neurotransmitters: Beyond dopamine, other neurotransmitters like serotonin and glutamate play a role in overthinking. Low levels of serotonin, linked to mood regulation, can contribute to anxious overthinking, while glutamate imbalances can further fuel intrusive thoughts.

Understanding the science behind overthinking is empowering. It helps us recognize that we're not broken or weak, but rather experiencing a complex interplay of evolutionary imprints and neurological processes. The good news? By acknowledging these forces and learning practical tools, we can begin to rewire our brains for less overthinking and more peace of mind. Stay tuned for the next chapter, where we'll explore powerful strategies to break free from the overthinking cycle and reclaim control of your mental landscape

Embracing a Journey of Change

Overthinking wasn't always your reality. Perhaps you remember a time when your mind flowed freely, unburdened by the constant hum of intrusive thoughts. But somewhere along the way, the cycle began, insidious and persistent. Now, overthinking feels like a heavy cloak, weighing down your spirit and stifling your joy. But amidst the struggle, a spark of hope remains. You wouldn't be reading this if you didn't yearn for something more, a breakthrough beyond the burden.

This book is your invitation to embark on a transformative journey, a path from the cramped quarters of overthinking to the expansive landscape of mindful awareness and empowered action. It's not a walk in the park, for change rarely is. But let me assure you, the destination is worth the effort. Imagine shedding the heavy cloak of overthinking and stepping into a life where:

- ❖ Peace of mind prevails. You silence the mental chatter, finding serenity in the present moment.
- ❖ Clarity guides your steps as you make decisions with confidence, unclouded by unnecessary worry.
- ❖ Resilience shields you and challenges no longer trigger anxiety spirals, but opportunities for growth.
- ❖ Unshackled from overthinking, your mind blossoms with imaginative possibilities.
- ❖ You connect authentically, present and engaged without the distraction of worry.

This transformation demands commitment, but the rewards are immeasurable. Imagine waking up each morning, not with the dread of overthinking, but with anticipation for a day filled with mindful presence and empowered action. Of course, you'll encounter hurdles, moments where the familiar pull of overthinking beckons. But remember, this journey is not about perfection; it's about progress, one step at a time.

This book is your guide on that journey. We'll delve into the science of overthinking, exposing its roots and mechanisms. We'll equip you with practical tools and techniques, from mindfulness practices to cognitive restructuring, to break free from its grip. We'll explore self-compassion and realistic expectations, crucial allies in this journey. You'll discover the power of identifying your triggers and creating strategies to interrupt the overthinking cycle.

So, take a deep breath, release the tension, and open your mind to the possibilities. This journey begins now, not with a destination in sight, but with a commitment to growth and the unwavering belief that you can transform. Are you ready to step out of the burden and embrace the breakthrough? Turn the page, and let's begin.

NB: There are little exercises that I'll ask you to do throughout the book. It'll help you in this journey so be sure to answer honestly.

Let's do a little exercise before we continue. Use this space to create a list of your core values. Things like integrity, family, creativity, health, or anything else you consider important.

<u>My Core Values</u>

____

____

____

____

____

____

____

____

____

____

PART 1: RECOGNIZING THE OVERTHINKING TRAP

Do you ever find yourself trapped in a mental labyrinth, endlessly replaying past conversations, dissecting decisions, and worrying about future possibilities? Welcome to the overthinking trap, a common yet insidious snare that steals our peace and productivity. Recognizing this trap is the first step towards freedom.

The signs are subtle, often mistaken for mere "thinking things through." In fact, a study on Rethinking Rumination shows that some people believe that they are doing well by going round their thoughts over and over again. But watch for telltale whispers: Does your mind become your worst critic, replaying negative scenarios on repeat? Does "analysis paralysis" grip you, preventing action? Do you feel drained and anxious after hours of mental rumination?

These whispers, if left unchecked, can morph into a roar, eroding your well-being. But don't despair! Recognizing the trap empowers you to break free. Mindfulness practices, gentle self-compassion, and setting realistic expectations are your allies. This section will go deep in discussing what exactly is overthinking and what the triggers are so you'll be aware.

Chapter 1: The Many Faces of Overthinking

Overthinking can feel like a faceless foe, an ever-present fog clouding your mind. But the reality is, that overthinking comes in many shapes and sizes, triggered by personal vulnerabilities and unique situations. Understanding your personal triggers is the first step to dismantling the overthinking machine and taking back control of your thoughts.

The Spectrum of Overthinking

Overthinking isn't always a constant barrage of negative thoughts. It can manifest in various ways, each with its own signature:

- → **Rumination**: Reliving past events, replaying conversations, fixating on mistakes.
- → **Catastrophizing**: Imagining worst-case scenarios, dwelling on potential failures.
- → **Mind-reading**: Attributing thoughts and motives to others without evidence, leading to anxiety.
- → **Shoulding**: Criticizing your actions and decisions, fueled by unrealistic expectations.
- → **Doubting**: Hesitating and second-guessing yourself, leading to missed opportunities.

From this spectrum, we'll now see the faces that overthinking can be in. Go through the lists and see if you recognise yourself in any.

Overthinking isn't a single, monolithic entity; it's a chameleon, adept at disguising itself in a multitude of forms. Sometimes it's a helpful planner, meticulously charting every step. Other times, it's a relentless critic, whispering doubts and anxieties in your ear. Recognizing these diverse faces of overthinking is key to understanding its impact and finding effective ways to manage it.

The Strategist: This overthinking persona meticulously plans every move, weighing every option and potential outcome. While this can be helpful in avoiding pitfalls, it can also lead to analysis paralysis, preventing action and hindering progress.

The Worrier: This face frets about the future, conjuring up worst-case scenarios and dwelling on potential problems. While some worry can be motivating, excessive worry breeds anxiety and steals joy from the present moment.

The Critic: This overthinker constantly judges themselves and others, replaying past mistakes and highlighting perceived flaws. This harsh inner voice can erode self-esteem and hinder healthy relationships.

The Perfectionist: This face sets impossibly high standards, striving for flawlessness in everything they do. While striving for excellence can be admirable, the relentless pursuit of perfection often leads to disappointment, frustration, and procrastination.

The Overanalyzer: This persona dissects every conversation, interaction, and event, replaying them in their mind and searching for hidden meanings. While some reflection can be valuable, excessive overanalyzing can drain mental energy and fuel unnecessary anxiety.

The Doubter: This overthinker constantly questions their decisions, accomplishments, and even their own worth. This pervasive doubt can hinder confidence and limit personal growth.

The Social Butterfly: This face overthinks every social interaction, worrying about what others think and replaying conversations long after they've ended. This can lead to social anxiety and avoidance, hindering meaningful connections.

The Planner: This overthinker meticulously plans every detail of their life, fearing deviation from the script. While some structures can be beneficial, rigid planning can stifle spontaneity and limit opportunities for growth and adaptation.

The Rehasher: This persona replays past mistakes and regrets, reliving negative experiences and dwelling on missed opportunities. This rumination can prevent moving forward and enjoying the present.

The What-If-er: This overthinker constantly imagines alternative scenarios, dwelling on "what ifs" and potential consequences. While some preparation is valuable, excessive what-if thinking can breed anxiety and prevent taking action.

These are just some of the many faces of overthinking. Recognizing your own patterns is the first step towards managing them. By understanding their underlying triggers and practicing mindfulness techniques, you can learn to navigate these mental pathways more effectively.

Chapter 2: The Cost of Constant Contemplation

Overthinking isn't just a harmless mental habit; it's a silent thief that robs us of our well-being in more ways than we realize. Like a persistent weed in a garden, it chokes life out of our joy, peace, and productivity, leaving us feeling depleted and disconnected.

While occasional deep thinking can be beneficial, overthinking often lurks in the shadows, casting a long and debilitating shadow on our mental and emotional well-being. Understanding these negative consequences is crucial to recognizing overthinking in yourself and taking steps to manage it effectively.

The Emotional Toll

Imagine living in a constant state of worry and self-doubt. Overthinking feeds anxiety, making us hypervigilant about potential threats and quick to interpret neutral situations negatively. This relentless negativity fosters feelings of worthlessness, inadequacy, and a constant sense of impending doom. The joy of the present moment gets swept away in the tide of worry about the past and fear of the future. Here are the ways it manifests and takes a toll on your emotional life.

- Anxiety and Stress: Ruminating on worries and replaying negative scenarios fuels anxiety and stress, leaving you feeling constantly on edge and drained.
- Depression and Hopelessness: Dwelling on past regrets and perceived failures can breed negativity and pessimism, contributing to feelings of depression and hopelessness.
- Diminished Self-Esteem: The harsh and critical voice of overthinking can chip away at your self-esteem, leading to insecurity and self-doubt.
- Decision Paralysis: Analyzing every option and consequence to the nth degree can make it impossible to make decisions, hindering progress and goal achievement.

The Physical Impact

Overthinking isn't just an emotional burden; it manifests in physical ways too. The stress hormones released during rumination wreak havoc on our bodies, leading to headaches, muscle tension, sleep disturbances, and even weakened immune systems. The constant fight-or-flight response takes a toll on our energy levels, leaving us feeling drained and exhausted. Overeating, neglecting exercise, and other unhealthy coping mechanisms can become tempting escapes, further impacting our physical health. Here are the ways it manifests.

- Sleep Problems: The worry and rumination associated with overthinking can disrupt sleep patterns, leading to insomnia and fatigue.
- Digestive Issues: The nervous system activation triggered by overthinking can impact digestion, leading to stomach aches and other digestive problems.
- Sleep Disruption: Worry and rumination interrupt sleep patterns, causing insomnia and fatigue.
- Physical Tension and Pain: Overthinking activates the stress response, leading to headaches, muscle tension, and other physical discomfort.

The Mental Fog

Overthinking clouds our mental clarity, making it difficult to focus, learn, and problem-solve effectively. It steals our creative spark, replacing it with mental exhaustion and decision paralysis. Our ability to make sound judgments gets impaired as we overanalyze every option, unable to trust our intuition or act decisively. This can lead to missed opportunities, career stagnation, and a general sense of feeling stuck in a mental rut.

- Depression and Hopelessness: Dwelling on past failures and regrets breeds negativity and pessimism, contributing to low mood and a sense of despair.
- Diminished Self-Esteem: The harsh inner critic of overthinking undermines self-confidence and leads to insecurity and self-doubt.
- Decision Paralysis: Overanalyzing every option and consequence hinders decision-making, hampering progress and goal achievement.
- Digestive Issues: Stress from over thinking can impact digestion, resulting in stomachaches and other problems.

Relationships suffer as overthinking fuels misunderstandings, misinterpretations, and communication breakdowns.

The Social Impact

Overthinking can have significant social ramifications, leading to strained relationships, missed opportunities, and decreased overall well-being. Constantly dwelling on past events or worrying about the future can hinder effective communication and connection with others. It may cause individuals to withdraw from social situations, fearing judgment or rejection. Overthinkers may struggle to make decisions, leading to indecisiveness and frustration among friends, family, and colleagues. This can lead to:

- Strained Relationships: Overthinking can lead to misinterpretations of others' actions and intentions, fostering mistrust and creating distance in relationships.
- Social Anxiety: Fear of judgment and negative evaluations from others can fuel social anxiety, hindering your ability to connect and enjoy social interactions.
- Isolation and Loneliness: When overthinking leads to social anxiety and avoidance, it can contribute to feelings of isolation and loneliness.

Beyond the Individual

The negative consequences of overthinking can extend beyond the individual, impacting:

- Work Performance: Overthinking can hinder productivity, creativity, and decision-making, impacting your performance at work.
- Quality of Life: The constant mental and emotional drain of overthinking can significantly reduce your overall quality of life and enjoyment of daily activities.
- Relationships with Others: When overthinking leads to anxiety, withdrawal, or misinterpretations, it can negatively impact

your relationships with family, friends, and colleagues.

Breaking Free from the Cycle
Knowing the cost of overthinking is the first step towards change. We must recognize it as a harmful pattern, not an innate part of our personalities. We have the power to change the situation, which is the positive aspect. By acknowledging its impact and actively seeking tools and strategies, we can reclaim our emotional, physical, and mental well-being.

But how did this overthinking endemic start? Who is to blame? In the upcoming chapter, we will delve into this matter further.

Chapter 3: Beyond the Blame Game

It's tempting to fall into the blame game when grappling with overthinking. But before pointing fingers at ourselves, let's take a step back and explore the complex tapestry of factors that contribute to overthinking tendencies. Understanding the roots, not assigning blame, empowers us to navigate this challenge with compassion and insight.

Evolutionary Whispers

Deep within our DNA lies an echo of our ancestors who navigated a world teeming with dangers. Their constant vigilance and analysis of potential threats might have ensured survival. However, in our relatively safer world, this "worry wart" tendency can manifest as overthinking, leading to unnecessary anxiety and rumination. Here are the exact ways our survival instinct helped to create overthinking.

☐ Hypervigilance: In our hunter-gatherer ancestors' world, vigilance against potential threats was crucial for survival. This ingrained pattern of scanning for danger can manifest as overthinking in modern times, where perceived threats might be more social or emotional.

- [ ] Planning and Problem-Solving: Carefully considering different scenarios and potential outcomes before taking action helped our ancestors avoid dangers and maximize opportunities. While beneficial in its original context, this tendency to overanalyze can become excessive in our complex and rapidly changing world.
- [ ] Social Navigation: Understanding the subtle cues and nuances of social interactions was vital for navigating complex tribal dynamics. This sensitivity can translate into overthinking social situations and ruminating on perceived slights or misinterpretations in the modern world.

Psychological Landscape

Personality traits like neuroticism, characterized by negative emotions and a tendency to worry, and high agreeableness, where pleasing others becomes a priority, can be linked to higher levels of overthinking. Additionally, experiences like childhood trauma, neglect, or critical environments can shape cognitive patterns that fuel rumination and negative self-talk.

Overthinking isn't simply a bad habit; it often stems from deeper psychological causes. Let's explore some key psychological contributors:

- [ ] Anxiety: Anxiety's constant "what if" scenarios and fear of the unknown can easily fuel overthinking as a coping mechanism, attempting to gain control through excessive planning and analyzing potential threats.

- [ ] Perfectionism: The relentless pursuit of flawlessness can lead to constant self-evaluation and overthinking every decision, fearing the slightest imperfection.

- [ ] Low Self-Esteem: When you doubt your worth and capabilities, you might overthink to compensate, seeking reassurance and validation through overanalyzing situations and interactions.

- [ ] Fear of Failure: Past experiences of failure or criticism can trigger a fear of repeating those mistakes, leading to overthinking as a way to avoid potential missteps.

- [ ] Fear of Judgment: An inflated fear of what others think can cause you to overthink social interactions, replay conversations and analyze perceived criticism.

- [ ] Obsessive-Compulsive Disorder (OCD): Intrusive thoughts and repetitive behaviors characteristic of OCD can manifest as excessive overthinking and rumination on specific themes or anxieties.

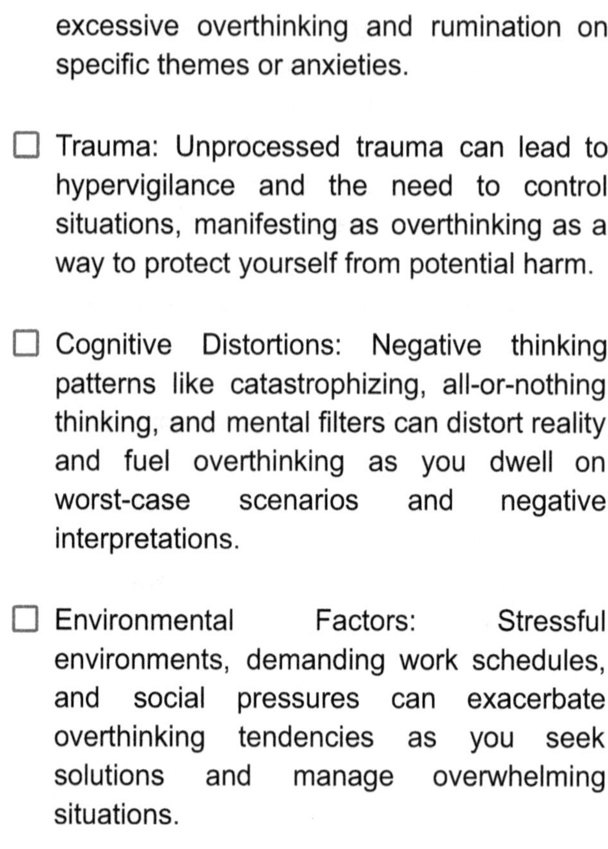

- ☐ Trauma: Unprocessed trauma can lead to hypervigilance and the need to control situations, manifesting as overthinking as a way to protect yourself from potential harm.

- ☐ Cognitive Distortions: Negative thinking patterns like catastrophizing, all-or-nothing thinking, and mental filters can distort reality and fuel overthinking as you dwell on worst-case scenarios and negative interpretations.

- ☐ Environmental Factors: Stressful environments, demanding work schedules, and social pressures can exacerbate overthinking tendencies as you seek solutions and manage overwhelming situations.

Cognitive Biases

Our brains are wired with certain biases that can distort our thinking and contribute to overthinking. The negativity bias makes us more attuned to potential threats and failures, while the confirmation bias seeks information that confirms our existing beliefs, even if negative. These biases can fuel overthinking by amplifying worries and making it difficult to see things objectively.

Our minds are marvelous, but not infallible. Cognitive biases, and systematic patterns of faulty thinking, can distort our perceptions and fuel the flames of overthinking. Recognizing these biases empowers us to challenge distorted thought patterns and navigate our mental landscape more effectively.

- ☐ Confirmation Bias: This bias seeks out information that confirms our existing beliefs, ignoring contradictory evidence. We overthink to find proof justifying our anxieties, reinforcing negative thought spirals.

- ☐ Negativity Bias: Our brains prioritize negative information, giving it more weight than positive experiences. This negativity bias fuels overthinking, dwelling on potential problems and overlooking the good.

- ☐ Availability Bias: The Availability Bias refers to our tendency to assess the probability of events based on the ease with which relevant examples come to our minds. Readily available memories of failures or negative experiences can fuel overthinking, skewing our perception of risk.

- [ ] Mental Filter: We selectively focus on specific details, often negative, while filtering out positive aspects. This filtering fuels overthinking, leading to distorted interpretations of situations and interactions.

- [ ] Catastrophizing: Jumping to worst-case scenarios and assuming negativity is a hallmark of this bias. Overthinking thrives on catastrophizing, magnifying potential problems and causing undue stress.

- [ ] All-or-nothing thinking: Seeing situations in extremes, with no shades of gray, fuels overthinking. We dwell on not achieving perfection or fearing complete failure, hindering progress and self-compassion.

- [ ] Should Statements: These internal pressures and rigid expectations create guilt and overthinking when not met. The notion of "I should be able to..." can impose a cognitive burden, leading to an overabundance of analysis and self-critique.

- [ ] Mind-Reading: Assuming we know others' thoughts and intentions, often negatively, fuels overthinking and misinterpretations. We create narratives, overthink their potential judgment, and build unnecessary anxieties.

Societal Pressures

The "cult of perfectionism" can create an environment where overthinking thrives. The constant comparison game fueled by social media and the fear of failure can make us hypercritical of ourselves and our actions, leading to rumination and self-doubt.

Overthinking doesn't exist in a vacuum. Societal pressures, like invisible threads, can weave themselves into our thought patterns, amplifying our tendencies to overthink and ruminate. Examining these external influences empowers us to understand their impact and create space for healthier mental frameworks.

- [ ] The Cult of Comparison: In today's hyper-connected world, bombarded by curated portrayals of success and happiness, comparing ourselves to others becomes almost inevitable. This constant comparison fuels self-doubt and overthinking, leading to anxieties about not measuring up and prompting excessive analysis of our own choices and outcomes.

- ☐ The Pressure to be "Perfect": Societal ideals of flawlessness and achievement can create an immense burden, pushing us to strive for unattainable perfection. This pressure fuels overthinking as we analyze every detail, seeking validation and fearing anything less than perfect.

- ☐ The Hustle Mentality: Glorifying constant busyness and productivity creates a sense of needing to be "on" all the time. This pressure leads to overthinking about maximizing every minute, fostering anxieties about falling behind and hindering relaxation and self-care, essential for mental well-being.

- ☐ The Fear of Missing Out (FOMO): The pervasive feeling of missing out on experiences or opportunities can trigger overthinking as we analyze social media feeds and compare our lives to others, leading to anxieties about making the "right" choices and hindering the enjoyment of the present moment.

- ☐ The Pressure to Conform: Societal expectations and norms can create anxieties about fitting in and avoiding disapproval. This fear of nonconformity fuels overthinking as we analyze every interaction and social encounter, fearing judgment and seeking acceptance.

☐ The Pressure to be Happy: The constant messaging to be happy and positive can paradoxically lead to overthinking our emotions. When happiness feels like a forced performance, we start scrutinizing our feelings, leading to rumination and self-doubt.

Understanding the roots of overthinking tendencies isn't about assigning blame; it's about creating awareness and self-compassion. Acknowledging the complex interplay of evolution, psychology, societal pressures, and our own experiences allows us to move beyond self-judgment and approach overthinking with understanding and acceptance.

The next chapters will equip you with practical tools and techniques to manage overthinking, not punish it. We'll explore mindfulness practices to quiet the mental chatter, cognitive restructuring to challenge negative thought patterns, and exposure therapy to confront fears head-on. We'll delve into building self-compassion, setting realistic expectations, and identifying triggers to break the overthinking cycle. Remember, you are not defined by your thoughts, and the power to create a life free from the tyranny of overthinking lies within you.

Chapter 4: Identifying Your Personal Triggers

Overthinking isn't a random phenomenon; it's often triggered by specific situations, emotions, or thoughts. Identifying these triggers empowers you to break free from its grip and cultivate a more mindful, present-moment awareness. By understanding your unique triggers, you can develop personalized strategies to interrupt overthinking patterns and reclaim control of your mental space.

Each of us has unique triggers that activate overthinking. By identifying yours, you'll be better equipped to anticipate and disarm them:

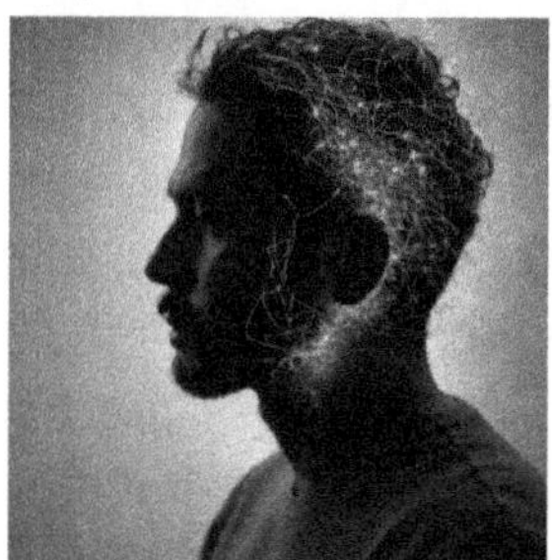

Situations: Do specific situations like deadlines, social interactions, or public speaking trigger overthinking?

Emotions: Do feelings like anxiety, anger, or sadness fuel overthinking cycles?

Internal dialogue: What kind of self-talk triggers overthinking? Self-criticism, comparisons, or perfectionist thoughts?

People: Are there specific interactions with people that spark overthinking?

Once you identify your triggers, you gain power. Here are some of the things you can do to equip yourself with tools to manage them. Do a self-appraisal and start with Self-Awareness. This will help you to track your thoughts and emotions: You can use the official workbook for this. It has all you need to keep a journal, noting down situations, emotions, and associated thoughts, especially when you find yourself overthinking. Identify any patterns or recurring themes.

You should also pay attention to the physical sensations around you. When do you normally feel the urge to overthink? Do you notice any physical cues like a racing heart, tense muscles, or shallow breathing? These may be early warning signs. Again, reflect on past experiences and think of any specific instances where you overthought. What triggered it? The workbook has all the spaces for you to use. You can also use your own journal to take note of these. It will help you to know your triggers.

Common Triggers to Explore

Here are some common triggers you need to know.

- Unclear situations or lack of control can spark anxieties and trigger overthinking as you try to analyze every possible outcome.
- Feeling stressed about work, academic performance, or social situations can lead to overthinking as you analyze your actions and worry about potential failures.
- Fear of judgment or rejection can trigger overthinking as you analyze the feedback and replay conversations, searching for flaws or hidden meanings.
- The relentless pursuit of flawlessness can fuel overthinking as you analyze every detail and worry about making mistakes.
- A harsh inner critic can trigger overthinking as you dwell on negative thoughts and self-doubts, creating a spiral of rumination.
- Comparing yourself to curated online portrayals of others can trigger overthinking and anxieties about not measuring up.
- When your mental and physical resources are depleted, you're more vulnerable to overthinking as your ability to manage emotions and thoughts gets compromised.

Identifying your triggers and developing coping mechanisms is a journey, not a destination. Be patient with yourself, celebrate your progress, and remember that you have the power to break free from the grip of overthinking and cultivate a more peaceful and mindful state of mind.

Let's continue with our little exercise. Use this space to reflect on why each of the values you listed before part 1, is important to you and how you prioritize these values in their lives.

<u>Why they are important to me</u>

PART 2: TOOLS AND TECHNIQUES FOR TRANSFORMATION

Overthinking isn't an insurmountable foe. With the right tools and techniques, you can transform your relationship with your thoughts and reclaim your peace of mind. This journey towards freedom isn't linear, but each step forward empowers you. Here's a glimpse into your toolkit:

Mindfulness Practices: Meditation, deep breathing, and mindful awareness exercises help ground you in the present, quieting the mental chatter and fostering self-compassion.

Cognitive Restructuring: Learn to challenge negative thought patterns, reframing them into more realistic and empowering perspectives.

Exposure Therapy: Gradually confront your fears and triggers in a safe environment, reducing their power and anxiety.

Identifying Triggers: Recognize situations, emotions, or self-talk that activate overthinking, allowing you to anticipate and manage them strategically.

Setting Realistic Expectations: Let go of perfectionism and embrace attainable goals, reducing self-criticism and fostering confidence.

Self-Compassion: Cultivate kindness and understanding towards yourself, acknowledging your struggles without judgment.

Healthy Coping Mechanisms: Find healthy ways to manage stress and anxiety, like exercise, creative pursuits, or spending time in nature.

Support Network: Surround yourself with understanding individuals who provide encouragement and healthy perspectives.

Chapter 5: Befriend Your Thoughts

Ever feel like your mind is a runaway train, hurtling through a landscape of worries and past regrets? If overthinking has become your unwelcome companion, mindfulness practices offer a powerful antidote. Imagine stepping off the train, observing the passing thoughts with detachment, and reclaiming control of your mental landscape. That's the essence of mindfulness: befriending your thoughts through awareness and acceptance, not judgment.

Understanding Mindfulness

Mindfulness, the practice of focusing your awareness on the present moment without judgment, offers a powerful tool for managing and reducing overthinking. It isn't about forcing your mind to be blank; it's about cultivating present-moment awareness without judgment. It's like observing your thoughts and emotions as passing clouds in the sky – acknowledging their presence without getting caught in their storm. This practice fosters inner peace, emotional regulation, and the ability to respond to situations with intention instead of being hijacked by automatic thoughts.

Understanding the Mechanism

When you overthink, your mind gets stuck in repetitive thought loops, often focused on the past or future. Mindfulness helps you disengage from these mental patterns by bringing your attention back to the present moment and your physical sensations, thoughts, and emotions as they arise. This change in perspective enables you to:

- Observe your thoughts and feelings without judgment. You start to see them as passing events, not defining truths.
- Reduce emotional reactivity. Instead of getting swept away by negative emotions, you learn to respond calmly and consciously.
- Increase self-awareness and become more attuned to your triggers and early signs of overthinking.
- Break the thought spiral by bringing your focus back to the present, you interrupt the cycle of rumination.

In essence, you are befriending your thoughts through mindfulness.

Meditation - Your Training Ground

Meditation is the cornerstone of mindfulness practice. Just like athletes train their bodies, meditation trains your mind to be present and focused. By sitting quietly and focusing on your breath, you cultivate the ability to observe your thoughts without getting entangled in them. There are various meditation techniques, from mindfulness meditation to guided meditations focusing on specific areas like gratitude or self-compassion. Find one that resonates with you and start with just a few minutes each day.

Befriending Your Thoughts

Mindfulness doesn't mean suppressing your thoughts; it's about observing them with curiosity and non-judgment. When you label a thought as "good" or "bad," you create resistance and reinforce its power. Instead, acknowledge its presence, say "hello," and let it go without getting attached. This fosters inner peace and reduces the power of overthinking.

Instead of making your thoughts your enemy, befriend them. Here are the exact practical steps you can use to befriend your thoughts through mindfulness in order to overcome overthinking.

- **Start with short practices:** Begin with 5-10 minutes of mindful breathing or meditation daily. Pay attention to your breath, the rise and fall of your chest, and any sensations in your body.
- **Practice throughout the day**: Take mindful moments throughout your day, like noticing the taste of your food, feeling your feet on the ground, or the sounds around you.
- **Recognize the urge to overthink**: When you catch yourself getting lost in thought,

gently bring your attention back to the present moment. Don't judge yourself, simply observe and redirect your focus.

- **Label your thoughts and feelings:** As thoughts arise, label them as "thinking" or "feeling anxious" without getting entangled in their content. This establishes distance between you and your thoughts.
- **Use your senses:** Engage your senses to ground yourself in the present. What do you see, hear, smell, taste, or touch? Focus on these details to anchor yourself in reality.
- **Practice guided meditations:** There are many guided meditations specifically designed to address overthinking. They can provide helpful prompts and techniques to practice mindfulness.

- **Be patient:** Learning mindfulness takes time and practice. Don't get discouraged if you find yourself getting drawn back into overthinking; simply bring your attention back with kindness and compassion.

Everyday Mindfulness

Mindfulness isn't confined to meditation cushions. The essence lies in interweaving mindfulness into the very fabric of your day-to-day experiences. Here are some practices to integrate mindfulness into everyday activities:

Mindful walking: Pay attention to your body sensations, the rhythm of your breath, and the sights and sounds around you as you walk.

Mindful eating: Savor each bite, noticing the taste, texture, and aroma of your food without distractions.

Mindful breathing: Take slow, deep breaths throughout the day to anchor yourself in the present moment.

Mindful body scans: Focus your attention on different parts of your body, noticing any tension or discomfort without judgment.

Chapter 6: Tame the Thought Storm

Imagine your mind as a swirling storm, fueled by negative thoughts and distorted beliefs. Overthinking thrives in this tempestuous environment, hijacking your emotions and clouding your judgment. But fear not, for within you lies the power to weather this storm – the power of cognitive restructuring.

Overthinking can feel like a relentless storm threatening to consume you. But just like any storm, it can be tamed. Here are some concrete steps to help you quiet the thought storm and reclaim control of your mind:

Step 1: Recognize the Storm
→ Pay attention to your triggers: Identify situations, emotions, or thoughts that typically trigger overthinking. Is it deadlines, social interactions, or uncertainty? Keep a mental or physical note to recognize them early.

→ Notice the signs: Be mindful of physical sensations like a racing heart, shallow breathing, or muscle tension. These can be early warnings of an impending thought storm.

Step 2: Take Cover

The moment you recognize a trigger or early sign, don't engage with the thoughts. Gently shift your focus away from them.

- → Engage your senses: Ground yourself in the present moment by engaging your senses. What do you see, hear, smell, taste, or touch right now? Focus on these details intently.
- → Practice mindful breathing: Take slow, deep breaths, focusing on the sensation of your breath entering and leaving your body. This has a soothing effect on the nervous system and promotes a sense of tranquility in the mind.

Step 3: Weather the Storm

Challenge negative thoughts: Don't accept your thoughts as facts. Question their validity and reframe them into more balanced and empowering perspectives. Are they based on evidence or just worries?

- → Label your emotions: Acknowledge your feelings without judgment. Saying "I feel anxious" can help detach from the emotion and observe it objectively.
- → Express yourself healthily: Write down your thoughts and feelings in a journal. Talking to a trusted friend or therapist can also be helpful.

Step 4: Rebuild After the Storm

→ Identify underlying issues: Reflect on what might be fueling your overthinking. Are there unresolved anxieties, perfectionism, or fear of failure? Addressing these can prevent future storms.

→ Develop coping mechanisms: Practice mindfulness and relaxation techniques regularly, making them your go-to tools for managing thoughts and emotions.

→ Seek professional help: If overthinking significantly impacts your daily life, consider seeking therapy. A therapist can equip you with personalized strategies and support.

Bonus Tips

Limit decision fatigue: Make small, unimportant decisions throughout the day to avoid feeling overwhelmed when faced with bigger choices.

Create a "worry time": If intrusive thoughts persist, designate a specific time each day to acknowledge and process them, then let them go during other times.

Understanding the Power of your Thoughts

Your thoughts aren't mere mental musings; they shape your emotions, behaviors, and ultimately, your reality. Overthinking thrives on distorted thinking patterns called cognitive distortions. These patterns, often formed in childhood or reinforced by experiences, act like faulty lenses, twisting our perception of reality and fueling negativity.

Common Cognitive Distortions
All-or-nothing thinking: Seeing situations in extremes, like "I failed this test, so I'm a complete failure."
Overgeneralization: Drawing broad conclusions from a single event, like "I made one mistake, so I'm always going to be bad at this."
Mental filtering: Focusing solely on negative information while ignoring positive aspects.
Mind reading: Assuming you know what others are thinking, often negatively.
Should statements: Creating unrealistic expectations for yourself and others, leading to self-criticism and frustration.

The Power of Restructuring

Cognitive restructuring is the art of identifying and challenging these distorted thought patterns. It's not about suppressing your thoughts, but about examining them critically and replacing them with more realistic and empowering perspectives. Think of it as replacing your faulty lenses with ones that offer a clearer, more objective view of reality.

Techniques for Restructuring

Identify the distortion: Recognize the specific cognitive distortions operating in your negative thought patterns.

Challenge the evidence: Is the evidence supporting your thought entirely accurate? Are you ignoring the positive aspects?

Consider alternative perspectives: What would someone else think of the situation? Would they view it more realistically?

Develop a more balanced and realistic thought: Replace the distorted thought with a more nuanced and empowering one.

Putting It into Practice

Let's say you're overthinking a mistake you made at work. You might think, "I'm such a failure, everyone thinks I'm incompetent." Here's how to restructure:

Identify the distortion: This is all-or-nothing thinking and mind reading.

Challenge the evidence: Did you make just one mistake, or do you consistently perform poorly? Do you have evidence that everyone thinks you're incompetent?

Consider alternative perspectives: Perhaps your colleagues understand everyone makes mistakes and are willing to help.

Develop a more balanced thought: "I made a mistake, but it doesn't define me. I can gain knowledge from the experience and improve in my future attempts."

Cognitive restructuring is a skill that takes practice. Don't lose hope if it doesn't yield perfect results initially. Remain patient, persistent, and acknowledge your achievements as you make progress. With consistent effort, you'll develop the mental agility to challenge negative thought patterns and replace them with empowering beliefs, ultimately taming the storm of overthinking.

In the following chapters, we'll explore other powerful tools and techniques to combat overthinking. We'll delve into how exposure therapy and building self-compassion can help you.

Chapter 7: Face Your Fears

Overthinking often thrives in the shadows, fueled by what-ifs and worst-case scenarios that play out in the safety of our minds. These imagined fears, while potentially paralyzing, rarely reflect reality. Exposure therapy, a powerful tool borrowed from cognitive-behavioral therapy (CBT), shines a light on these shadows, helping you confront your fears head-on and break the rumination cycle.

While overthinking can offer some benefits in planning and problem-solving, it often crosses the line into debilitating worry and rumination. Facing your fears, instead of dwelling on them, can be a powerful way to break free from the cycle of overthinking and cultivate a more confident and empowered life. Here's how:

Overthinking often stems from fear: fear of failure, judgment, the unknown, or potential negative consequences. By avoiding situations that trigger these fears, we reinforce the overthinking patterns. Facing your fears, however, challenges these avoidance tendencies and can lead to several positive outcomes:

Reduced anxiety and worry: As you successfully confront your fears, you gain confidence and evidence that you can handle challenging situations. This reduces the need for excessive overthinking.

Increased self-efficacy: Stepping outside your comfort zone demonstrates your capabilities and strengthens your belief in your ability to overcome challenges.

Greater exposure and desensitization: Facing your fears in small, manageable steps gradually reduces their power over you, ultimately leading to less emotional reactivity and less need for overthinking.

Personal growth and resilience: Embracing challenges and overcoming obstacles fosters personal growth and builds resilience, making you better equipped to navigate future anxieties.

Start Small and Gradually Progress: Facing your fears doesn't mean jumping into the deep end. Begin with small, manageable steps that feel slightly uncomfortable but not overwhelming. Here's how to approach it gradually:

- Pinpoint the specific situations or thoughts that trigger overthinking. Be honest and specific about what scares you.
- Rank your fears from least to most anxiety-provoking. This helps you start with the most manageable ones and build confidence gradually.
- Divide large fears into smaller, more achievable steps. For example, if you fear public speaking, start by giving a short presentation to a small group of trusted friends.

- Acknowledge and commemorate each and every stride you make, regardless of its magnitude. Keep in mind that conquering fear is an ongoing expedition, rather than a final endpoint.

Tips for Successful Fear-Facing

- Techniques like meditation and deep breathing can help manage anxiety and maintain focus as you face your fears.
- Imagine yourself successfully overcoming your fear in a safe and supportive environment. This positive visualization can boost confidence and reduce nervousness.
- After each successful step, reward yourself with something you enjoy. This reinforces positive behavior and motivates you to keep going.
- Don't be discouraged if you experience setbacks. They are a normal part of the process. Learn from them and try again.

Understanding Exposure Therapy

Imagine your fear of public speaking as a monster lurking in the dark. By staying in the shadows, and avoiding presentations, you empower the monster. Exposure therapy brings the monster into the light, gradually exposing you to it in a safe and controlled environment. As you face your fear repeatedly, its power diminishes, and so does your anxiety.

Applying Exposure Therapy to Overthinking
Overthinking thrives on avoidance. You ruminate on potential failures, social awkwardness, or negative judgments, all without actually experiencing them. Exposure therapy challenges this avoidance in three key ways:

Identifying Triggers: Begin by pinpointing the situations or topics that trigger your overthinking. Is it public speaking, making decisions, or interacting with specific people?
Gradual Exposure: Start with small, manageable exposures. If public speaking is your fear, begin by reading aloud to a friend, then progress to small presentations.
Repeat and Observe: Repeat each exposure level multiple times. As you do, observe how your anxiety decreases and your confidence increases.

Breaking the Rumination Cycle
Exposure therapy disrupts the vicious cycle of overthinking. By facing your fears in a safe space, you gather evidence that contradicts your negative predictions. This weakens the power of your worries and reduces the urge to ruminate. Additionally, exposure therapy teaches you coping mechanisms to manage anxiety during real-life situations, further reducing the need for overthinking.

Exposure therapy isn't about instant cures; it's a gradual process that requires commitment and self-compassion. There will be moments of discomfort, but celebrate your progress, no matter how small. Each step forward weakens the grip of overthinking and empowers you to live a life less dictated by fear and more guided by courage and confidence.

In the coming chapters, we'll explore other tools and techniques to combat overthinking, including self-compassion, setting realistic expectations, and building resilience. You have the strength and resources to break free from the cycle of overthinking and create a life filled with peace, clarity and purpose.

Chapter 8: Love Yourself

In the battle against overthinking, we often resort to self-criticism and blame. We view our overthinking tendencies as flaws, fueling a cycle of negativity and frustration. But what if the key to breaking free wasn't self-punishment, but self-compassion? Imagine facing your overthinking with the same kindness and understanding you offer a dear friend – that's the essence of self-compassion, and it holds immense power in curbing overthinking's grip.

Cultivating self-love can be a powerful weapon against overthinking. When you truly love and accept yourself, your inner critic quiets, and the need to overanalyze every thought and action diminishes. Here's how self-love can help you silence the overthinking storm:

The Link Between Self-Love and Overthinking
Reduced self-doubt: Overthinking often stems from insecurities and questioning your worth. Self-love fosters self-confidence and inner peace,

reducing the need for constant reassurance and validation through overthinking.

More compassion: When you love yourself, you become more understanding and forgiving of your imperfections. This reduces the harsh self-criticism that fuels rumination and negative thought spirals.

Greater acceptance: Self-love encourages you to accept your thoughts and feelings without judgment, letting go of the need to control everything through overthinking.

Focus on the present: Self-love allows you to appreciate the present moment and your true self, instead of getting lost in worries about the past or future.

Steps to Cultivate Self-Love

→ Practice Self-Compassion: Talk to yourself the way you would talk to a dear friend. Acknowledge your struggles without judgment and offer yourself kindness and understanding.

→ Identify and challenge negative self-talk: Pay attention to your inner critic and actively challenge its negativity. Replace negative thoughts about oneself with positive affirmations and constructive self-talk.

→ Celebrate your strengths and accomplishments: Take time to appreciate your unique qualities and achievements, big or small. Focusing on your strengths boosts your self-esteem and reduces the need for self-doubt.

→ Engage in activities you enjoy: Prioritize activities that bring you joy and fulfillment, nurturing your physical and mental well-being.

→ Set healthy boundaries: Learn to say no to things that drain your energy or violate your values. Respecting your needs fosters self-love and reduces stress, which can trigger overthinking.

→ Connect with supportive people: Surround yourself with people who appreciate and uplift you. Their positive energy can counter negative self-talk and promote self-acceptance.

→ Practice gratitude: Expressing gratitude for the good things in your life, big or small, shifts your focus to the positive and reduces negativity, a key driver of overthinking.

→ Seek professional help: If you struggle with self-love, consider therapy or support groups. A therapist can help you identify negative patterns and develop strategies for building self-compassion and acceptance.

As you nourish your self-love, you'll find yourself overthinking less and living more authentically in the present moment.

Understanding Self-Compassion

Self-compassion isn't about self-pity or condoning unhealthy behaviors. It's about acknowledging your struggles with kindness and understanding, recognizing that overthinking is a common human experience and not a mark of failure. It's about treating yourself with the same warmth and support you readily offer others.

Why is Self-Compassion Important for Overthinking?

Self-criticism fuels the fire of overthinking. When we judge ourselves harshly for every negative thought, we create an internal conflict that reinforces rumination. Self-compassion, on the other hand, offers a soothing balm. It allows us to observe our thoughts with detachment, accepting them as temporary blips on the screen of our minds, not defining truths about ourselves.

Building self-compassion is a journey, not a destination. Here are some guidelines to support you:

- Mindfulness cultivates self-awareness, allowing you to observe your thoughts and feelings without judgment. This creates space to respond with kindness instead of reactivity.
- Replace self-critical inner chatter with encouraging and understanding phrases.

Talk to yourself as you would to a loved one facing a difficulty.
- Remind yourself that everyone experiences negative thoughts and struggles. You have a community of people who understand, and your challenges are legitimate.
- Let go of past mistakes and perceived shortcomings. Forgive yourself as you would forgive a friend who made a mistake.
- This practice, where you send well-wishes to yourself and others, cultivates warmth and compassion towards yourself.

Self-Compassion and Overthinking

As you cultivate self-compassion, you'll notice a shift in your relationship with overthinking. You'll be less likely to get swept away by negative thoughts and more able to observe them with detachment. This reduces their power and allows you to choose more helpful responses.

Self-compassion isn't just about feeling good; it translates into action. Be kind to yourself in your actions: prioritize sleep, healthy eating, and activities that bring you joy. Set realistic goals and celebrate your progress, not just your achievements. Extend to yourself the same level of respect and care that you extend to others.

Building self-compassion takes time and practice. There will be moments when self-criticism creeps in, but don't be discouraged. Gently remind yourself of your worth and keep practicing self-kindness. With consistent effort, self-compassion will become a powerful ally in your journey to overcome overthinking and create a life filled with more peace, acceptance, and self-love.

Start small and focus on daily acts of self-care. Take a relaxing bath, read a good book, enjoy a healthy meal, or spend time in nature. These small acts of self-love accumulate, gradually fostering a deeper sense of appreciation and acceptance for yourself.

By choosing self-love, you take a powerful step towards silencing the overthinking storm and reclaiming a life filled with peace, confidence, and joy. You deserve it!

In the next chapter, we'll explore setting realistic expectations, building resilience, and creating a support network – all crucial aspects of your journey towards a life free from the grip of overthinking. Remember, you are not alone. You have the strength and resources to break free and create a life filled with peace, clarity, and purpose.

Chapter 9: Setting Realistic Expectations

Overthinking often thrives on a distorted lens through which we view ourselves and the world. Unattainable goals, societal pressures, and the relentless comparison game fuel anxiety and dissatisfaction, creating a breeding ground for rumination and negativity.

But what if the key to breaking free wasn't pushing harder, but shifting our perspective? This chapter invites you to explore the power of setting realistic expectations, redefining success on your own terms, and embracing imperfection as a stepping stone, not a stumbling block.

The Tyranny of Unrealistic Expectations
We often set expectations based on external pressures, societal norms, or unrealistic comparisons. The desire to live up to these externally imposed standards fuels a constant internal struggle, leaving us feeling inadequate and defeated. When these expectations collide with reality, the disappointment breeds overthinking and self-doubt, perpetuating the cycle.

Setting realistic expectations is a crucial tool for breaking free from the cycle of overthinking and cultivating a more peaceful mind. When our expectations are unrealistic, we set ourselves up for disappointment and constant comparisons, fueling rumination and negative thought patterns. Here's how establishing practical expectations can be beneficial:

Understanding the Power of Expectation

Realistic expectations prevent you from setting yourself up for failure, minimizing the disappointment and frustration that trigger overthinking. When goals are achievable, you're more likely to feel motivated and take action, reducing the need for excessive planning and mental rehearsal.

By accepting limitations and appreciating the process, you become more forgiving of yourself, diminishing the harsh self-criticism that fuels overthinking. Realistic expectations keep your attention anchored in the present, where you can take concrete steps towards achieving your goals, instead of getting lost in worries about the future.

Steps to Set Realistic Expectations
- Discover your core values: Determine what holds utmost importance to you in life. Define your core values and goals to guide your expectations. This is where the values you listed in the previous pages, before part 1, comes in handy.

- Consider your resources: Be honest about your time, energy, skills, and limitations. Setting goals beyond your means is a recipe for overthinking and frustration.
- Research and gather information: Learn about the average outcomes in your desired areas. Aiming for the absolute best isn't always realistic or healthy.
- Start small and build gradually: Don't overwhelm yourself with too much too soon. Break down large goals into smaller, achievable steps, celebrating each milestone along the way.
- Be flexible and adaptable: Life throws curveballs. Be willing to adjust your expectations when necessary, focusing on progress over perfection.
- Celebrate the journey: Enjoy the process of learning and growing, not just the end result. This reduces the pressure to achieve unrealistic outcomes and minimizes the need for overthinking.

Tips for Success

Ask trusted friends, mentors, or colleagues for their honest assessment of your goals and expectations. Their insights can help you adjust your thinking.

Focusing on what you have and appreciating your progress fosters contentment and reduces the need for comparisons and unrealistic expectations.

Imagine yourself achieving your goals in a realistic and manageable way. This positive visualization can boost motivation and reduce anxieties about unrealistic outcomes.

If setting realistic expectations is challenging, consider therapy. A therapist can help you identify underlying beliefs and patterns that might be hindering your progress.

True success isn't a fixed destination; it's a personal journey guided by your values, passions, and aspirations. What truly matters to you? Fulfillment, growth, connection, contribution? Redefine success based on these internal markers, not external validation. What does achieving success look like on your own terms?

Embracing Imperfection

Striving for flawlessness fuels anxiety and overthinking. Perfectionism creates a rigid mental landscape where any misstep feels catastrophic. The truth is, imperfection is inherent to the human experience. Mistakes are bound to happen, but they provide valuable chances for growth and learning. Embrace imperfection as a natural part of your journey, and release the burden of needing to be perfect.

Setting Realistic Goals

Ambition is valuable, but unrealistic goals set you up for disappointment and fuel overthinking. BDivide your goals into smaller, attainable tasks to make them more manageable. Celebrate progress, however small, and acknowledge the effort behind each accomplishment.

The Ripple Effect
Redefining success and embracing imperfection have a ripple effect. As you release the pressure of unrealistic expectations, you'll experience:

Reduced anxiety and overthinking: When you stop striving for unattainable ideals, your mind calms and your ability to focus sharpens.
Increased motivation: Realistic goals feel achievable, fueling motivation and persistence.
Self-compassion and acceptance: Embracing imperfection fosters self-love and a kinder inner dialogue.
Greater authenticity: Living by your own standards allows you to express your true self with confidence.

Shifting your mindset and setting realistic expectations is a continuous process. There will be days when old patterns resurface, but don't be discouraged. Gently remind yourself of your chosen path, celebrate your progress, and extend compassion to yourself throughout the journey.

This journey doesn't end here. Remember, you are not alone in this quest to break free from the shackles of overthinking and create a life filled with peace, purpose, and self-acceptance. Keep exploring, keep growing, and keep reminding yourself: that you are worthy, just as you are, on this imperfect and beautiful journey called life.

Chapter 10: Use Interruption Strategies

You've explored the roots of overthinking, equipped yourself with powerful tools, and redefined your relationship with expectations. Now comes the crucial step: actively interrupting overthinking cycles before they take hold. By identifying your triggers and implementing effective strategies, you can reclaim control of your thoughts and reclaim your peace of mind.

Overthinking can be like a runaway train, but interruption strategies can be the emergency brakes. Here are some steps to help you stop overthinking, using different interruption techniques:

1. Recognize the overthinking
Catch yourself. Notice when your mind is replaying scenarios, dwelling on the negative, or going down unhelpful rabbit holes. Pay attention to physical cues like muscle tension or racing thoughts.

2. Choose your interruption strategy
External Distraction:
- Engage your senses: Go for a walk, listen to music, do some stretching, take a shower. Ground yourself in the present moment.
- Start an activity: Do a puzzle, work on a hobby, read a book, clean your room. Engage your mind in something productive.

- Socialize: Talk to a friend, call family, play with your pet. Connect with others to shift your focus.

<u>Internal Shift:</u>
- Challenge your thoughts: Ask yourself if your thoughts are realistic, helpful, or based on evidence. Challenge negative self-talk with positive affirmations.
- Label your thoughts: Say to yourself, "This is just a thought, not necessarily reality." Observe your thoughts without judgment, like passing clouds.
- Mindfulness techniques: Practice deep breathing, meditation, or guided imagery to bring your attention to the present moment.

3. Take Action
- Set a time limit: If you need to think about something specific, schedule a dedicated "worry time" for 10-15 minutes. After that, move on.
- Take a small step: If you're overthinking a decision, choose the simplest action you can take to move forward. Progress often beats perfection.
- Seek assistance: Engage in conversations with a therapist, counselor, or a reliable confidant. They can help you develop coping mechanisms and challenge unhelpful thought patterns.

Be patient. Interrupting overthinking takes practice. Don't get discouraged if it doesn't work perfectly at first. Experiment with different strategies until you find ones that resonate with you. Acknowledge your efforts and small wins. Remember, conquering overthinking is a continuous process rather than a final goal.

Know Your Enemy

The first step is understanding what sparks your overthinking. Do specific situations, emotions, or people trigger anxious rumination? Journaling, mindfulness practice, and self-reflection can help you uncover these patterns. Identifying your triggers empowers you to anticipate them and prepare your response. Also, seeking support. Talk to a trusted friend, therapist, or support group for encouragement and different perspectives.

Distraction Techniques: Engage in activities that require focused attention, like exercise, hobbies, or spending time in nature, to shift your mental focus. Positive Affirmations: Counter negative thoughts with positive self-talk, reminding yourself of your strengths and capabilities.

The most effective strategies are the ones that resonate with you. Experiment with different techniques and find what works best in different situations. Remember, consistency is key. The more you practice interrupting overthinking, the stronger your mental muscle becomes.

Develop a personalized toolkit filled with your chosen interruption strategies. Keep it readily available for moments when you feel the familiar pull of overthinking. This could be a list of mindfulness exercises, positive affirmations, or contact information for your support network.

Breaking the overthinking cycle isn't about achieving perfection; it's about progress. There will be setbacks, moments when old patterns resurface. Don't get discouraged. Acknowledge the slip, practice self-compassion, and gently redirect your attention back to your chosen strategies. With consistent effort and self-kindness, you'll gradually weaken the grip of overthinking and create a life filled with greater presence, peace, and empowered action.

Continue nurturing self-compassion, setting realistic expectations, and exploring new tools and techniques for managing stress and anxiety. Celebrate your progress, embrace your imperfections, and keep moving forward on your path to freedom from overthinking.

Let's continue with our little exercise. Use this space to identify situations where you've felt most aligned with your values and times when you've felt a sense of conflict.

<u>**What Happened**</u>

____

____

____

____

____

____

____

____

____

____

"The only thing more dangerous than overthinking is believing that there is something to think about."

\-

Thomas Wharton

PART 3: EMBRACING A LIFE BEYOND OVERTHINKING

Overthinking can feel like a constant companion, but it doesn't have to define you. This journey has equipped you with tools and strategies to break free. Remember, it's a marathon, not a sprint. Be kind to yourself, celebrate progress, and keep practicing. As you quiet the mental chatter and embrace mindful awareness, you'll discover a life filled with:

Greater peace. Less rumination means less anxiety and more inner calm.
Enhanced clarity. Focus on the present instead of getting lost in worries.

Empowered action. Make decisions with confidence, taking steps guided by intention, not overthinking.

Deeper connections. Authentic interactions flourish when you're truly present in the moment.

Self-compassion. Embrace your imperfections and extend kindness to yourself, fostering self-acceptance.

In the following chapters, you will learn habits that will sustain all you've learned so that overthinking will be a thing of the past for you. You will learn how to build resilience, combat stress, cultivate gratitude and create a supportive ecosystem.

Chapter 11: Build Resilience

Overthinking thrives in the cracks of our resilience. When life throws curveballs, the tendency to ruminate intensifies, amplifying stress and robbing us of the ability to bounce back. But within you lies a wellspring of resilience, waiting to be tapped. This chapter guides you towards nurturing your inner resources and building a powerful stress management toolkit to navigate life's inevitable challenges with greater ease and composure.

Resilience isn't about avoiding challenges; it's about navigating them with strength, flexibility, and adaptability. It's the ability to bend without breaking, bouncing back from setbacks and emerging stronger. Cultivating resilience empowers you to manage stress effectively, reducing the triggers for overthinking and fostering overall well-being.

Building Your Inner Arsenal
Here are some **key resources to strengthen your resilience**:

- ❖ Practice mindfulness meditation, deep breathing exercises, or progressive muscle relaxation to cultivate inner calm and manage stress in the moment.
- ❖ Prioritize sleep, healthy eating, and regular exercise. Your body and mind are interconnected; taking care of one strengthens the other.

❖ Challenge negative thought patterns and cultivate a kinder internal dialogue. Reaffirm your abilities and previous achievements to enhance your self-assurance.

❖ Surround yourself with supportive and understanding individuals who provide encouragement and different perspectives.

❖ Meaning and Purpose: Identify your values and connect them to activities that bring meaning and purpose to your life. This determination instills drive and perseverance.

❖ Cultivate an attitude of gratitude by focusing on the positive aspects of your life, even during challenging times.

❖ If you're struggling to manage stress or overcome overthinking, don't hesitate to seek professional help from a therapist or counselor.

Remember, these are just starting points. Explore different practices and discover what resonates most with you. Consistency is key – the more you integrate these practices into your daily life, the stronger your resilience becomes.

Stress Management Strategies
In addition to building inner resources, equip yourself with practical stress management strategies:

Identify and Address Stressors: Pay attention to situations or people that trigger your stress response. Find healthy ways to address them or create boundaries if necessary.

Time management: This involves planning and prioritizing tasks in order to prevent feeling overwhelmed. It is important to delegate tasks whenever possible and to learn how to politely decline additional commitments in order to avoid overcommitting oneself.

Problem-Solving Skills: Develop healthy coping mechanisms for dealing with challenges. Break down problems into manageable steps and focus on finding solutions instead of dwelling on negativity.

Seeking Support: Don't be afraid to ask for help from friends, family, or professionals when you feel overwhelmed.

Building resilience is a lifelong journey. There will be times when stress and overthinking resurface. Don't be discouraged. View these moments as opportunities to practice your self-care, implement your stress management strategies, and reach out for support. With ongoing effort and self-compassion, you'll build an inner strength that allows you to navigate life's challenges with greater grace and ease, leaving overthinking behind in the dust.

As this journey continues, remember, you are not alone. Overcoming overthinking is a testament to your courage and commitment to personal growth. Keep exploring, keep learning, and keep moving forward on your path to a life filled with peace, clarity, and empowered action. You have the tools and resources you need to create a life you truly love, free from the shackles of overthinking. Go forth and conquer!

Chapter 12: Cultivate Gratitude

As we conclude this journey towards breaking free from overthinking, let's shift our focus from managing mental noise to nurturing a powerful antidote: gratitude. By cultivating an appreciative lens, we unlock a treasure trove of inner peace, resilience, and joy, ultimately leaving overthinking behind in the dust. Cultivating gratitude can indeed serve as a powerful antidote for overthinking.

The Power of Gratitude
Gratitude isn't just about saying "thank you"; it's a conscious shift in perspective, a decision to focus on the positive aspects of life, big and small. This practice rewires our neural pathways, fostering optimism, reducing stress, and boosting overall well-being. It acts as a shield against overthinking, redirecting our attention from worries to the abundance already present. Here's how:

Shifts Focus

Practicing gratitude helps shift your focus away from negative thoughts and worries by redirecting your attention to the positive aspects of your life.

Promotes Mindfulness

Gratitude encourages you to be present in the moment and appreciate the here and now, reducing rumination on past events or anxious thoughts about the future.

Fosters Positivity

By acknowledging and appreciating the blessings in your life, gratitude fosters a more positive outlook, which can counteract pessimism and self-doubt associated with overthinking.

Increases Resilience

Regularly expressing gratitude strengthens your resilience to stress and adversity, making it easier to cope with challenges and setbacks without spiraling into excessive rumination.

Enhances Perspective

Gratitude broadens your perspective, helping you see beyond your immediate concerns and recognize the bigger picture. This broader view can diminish the significance of minor worries and reduce overthinking.

Improves Self-Esteem

Practicing gratitude boosts self-esteem and self-worth by highlighting your strengths and accomplishments, which can counteract feelings of inadequacy or self-criticism that fuel overthinking.

Promotes Sleep and Well-Being

Gratitude has been linked to improved sleep quality and overall well-being, as it fosters a sense of peace and contentment that can alleviate the restlessness and anxiety often associated with overthinking.

To cultivate gratitude as an antidote for overthinking, consider incorporating daily gratitude practices into your routine, such as keeping a gratitude journal, expressing appreciation to others, or simply taking a moment every day to contemplate the things you appreciate. Over time, you'll likely find that practicing gratitude helps quiet your overactive mind and brings a greater sense of peace and contentment to your life.

Developing a Gratitude Practice

The good news is, that gratitude can be cultivated just like any other skill. Here are a few techniques to help you begin:

Gratitude Journaling: Dedicate 5-10 minutes each day to reflect on things you're grateful for. Jot down big wins, small moments of joy, or simply the basic blessings of life.

Gratitude Jar: Write down things you're grateful for on slips of paper and keep them in a jar. Draw one out each day as a reminder of your blessings.

Mindful Appreciation: During daily activities, pause to appreciate the beauty around you – the warmth of the sun, the taste of your food, the laughter of loved ones.

Gratitude Meditation: Guided meditations specifically focused on cultivating gratitude can deepen your practice and its benefits.

Expressing Gratitude: Tell people you appreciate them, whether it's a heartfelt thank you note, a genuine compliment, or simply expressing your affection.

Remember, gratitude isn't a forced feeling; it's a shift in perspective. Start small, be genuine, and don't get discouraged if negativity creeps in. Acknowledge it, gently redirect your focus, and keep practicing. Consistency is key, and over time, gratitude will become a natural lens through which you experience life.

The Impact on Overthinking

As you cultivate gratitude, you'll notice a remarkable shift. Overthinking thrives on negativity, but gratitude starves it of fuel. By appreciating what you have, you reduce the space for worries and rumination. You become more present in the moment, savoring the good instead of dwelling on the "what-ifs."

Gratitude and Beyond
Gratitude isn't just an antidote to overthinking; it's a foundation for a fulfilling life. When you appreciate what you have, you become more open to receiving abundance, fostering stronger relationships, and experiencing greater joy. You become more resilient in the face of challenges, finding the silver lining even in difficult times.

This journey doesn't end here. Embrace gratitude as a lifelong practice, a continuous act of nurturing your well-being. Go forth, spread gratitude, and remember, you are worthy of all the good things life has to offer.

Chapter 13: Creating a Supportive Ecosystem

You've conquered the chapters, tackled the tools, and cultivated inner resources. Yet, your journey towards freedom from overthinking isn't a solo expedition. Building a supportive ecosystem – nurturing healthy relationships and seeking help when needed – becomes your final compass, guiding you towards lasting change and empowered well-being.

The Power of Connection
Humans are social creatures, wired for connection. Surrounding ourselves with supportive individuals can significantly impact our mental and emotional well-being. These positive relationships act as a buffer against stress, offering encouragement, acceptance, and different perspectives. They can be a sounding board for your struggles, a source of celebration for your victories, and a safe space to practice vulnerability and self-compassion.

Finding Your Tribe
Not everyone in your life needs to be a close confidante. Seek out individuals who share your values, and interests, and who genuinely uplift you. Join clubs, groups, or activities that align with your passions, fostering a sense of belonging and community. Remember, quality over quantity – a

few genuine connections can make a world of difference.

Building Healthy Relationships

Healthy relationships aren't one-sided; they require effort and intention. Here are some ways to nurture them:

Prioritize quality time: Spend meaningful time with your loved ones, engaging in activities you both enjoy.
Practice active listening: Give your full attention when others speak, showing genuine interest and empathy.
Offer support and encouragement: Be there for your loved ones during their challenges, and celebrate their successes.
Communicate openly and honestly: Express your thoughts and feelings authentically, while respecting the perspectives of others.
Set healthy boundaries: Establish clear boundaries to protect your well-being and maintain healthy dynamics.

Seeking Professional Help:
Sometimes, even with a supportive network, professional guidance can be invaluable. Don't hesitate to seek help from a therapist, counselor, or coach if you feel overwhelmed, stuck, or need

additional support in managing overthinking or other mental health concerns.

Finding the Right Fit
Finding the right therapist or counselor is crucial. Consider their speciality, approach, and personality fit. Don't be afraid to interview potential professionals until you find someone you feel comfortable and safe with.

Building a supportive ecosystem is a continuous process. There will be times when relationships require effort, communication, and even forgiveness. Be patient with yourself and others, and remember, you deserve healthy connections and access to professional support when needed.

The Ripple Effect
As you nurture healthy relationships and seek help when needed, you'll experience a ripple effect. You will have reduced stress and anxiety. This is because supportive connections and professional guidance can equip you with better coping mechanisms, leading to reduced stress and anxiety.

You will feel valued and supported by others bolsters your sense of self-worth and confidence. Talking to a therapist or counselor can help you gain deeper insights into your thoughts, feelings, and triggers.

By practicing healthy communication in your relationships, you become more adept at expressing yourself and understanding others. As you continue your journey, cherish the connections that uplift you, embrace the courage to seek help when needed, and remember:

You are worthy of love and support. It is crucial to prioritize your mental well-being. You have the strength and resources to navigate challenges.

Your journey towards empowered well-being is ongoing, and every step forward matters. Go forth, build your supportive ecosystem, and continue to create a life free from the grip of overthinking. Keep in mind that you possess inner strength and resilience beyond your imagination. Embrace this unique journey of yours, for it is truly magnificent.

Chapter 14: Celebrating Your Progress

In the journey of personal growth and development, it's easy to get caught up in the pursuit of goals and forget to acknowledge the milestones along the way. This chapter is dedicated to the importance of celebrating your progress, no matter how small, and the power of recognizing and rewarding your victories.

Acknowledging Your Achievements
Before you can celebrate your progress, you must first acknowledge your achievements. This section encourages readers to reflect on their journey and take inventory of the milestones they've reached. From overcoming obstacles to mastering new skills, each achievement deserves recognition.

The Power of Celebration
Celebrating your progress isn't just about throwing a party or indulging in treats—it's about acknowledging your hard work and giving yourself the credit you deserve. This section explores the psychological benefits of celebration, including increased motivation, confidence, and resilience.

Ways to Celebrate
From simple gestures to grand gestures, there are countless ways to celebrate your progress. This section offers practical suggestions for how readers

can reward themselves, such as treating themselves to a spa day, indulging in their favorite meal, or taking a well-deserved vacation.

Creating Rituals

To make celebrating progress a regular part of your journey, it's essential to create rituals that honor your achievements. This section encourages readers to establish meaningful traditions, such as journaling about their victories, creating vision boards, or sharing their successes with loved ones.

The Importance of Self-Compassion
While celebrating progress is important, it's also crucial to practice self-compassion when setbacks occur. You should know that setbacks are a natural part of the journey and encourage them to treat themselves with kindness and understanding during challenging times.

This chapter concludes with a reminder of the importance of celebrating progress as a way to stay motivated, build confidence, and cultivate a positive mindset. By recognizing and rewarding your victories, you can fuel your continued growth and embrace the journey with joy and gratitude.

Conclusion

You've reached the culmination of this empowering journey. As you close this book, remember you've not just read words; you've embarked on a transformation. You've challenged the grip of overthinking, explored powerful tools, and built a foundation for lasting change. Now, it's time to integrate these learnings and step forward with newfound confidence and clarity.

Reframing Your Mindset
Overthinking often stems from distorted thinking patterns. Remember the tools you've gained: cognitive restructuring, mindfulness, and self-compassion. Use them to challenge negative thoughts, cultivate present-moment awareness, and treat yourself with kindness. As you reframe your mindset, you'll see the world and yourself through a more empowering lens.

Reclaiming Your Life
Just know that overthinking doesn't define you. You are capable, worthy, and deserving of a life filled with peace, purpose, and joy. Use the tools you've acquired to make decisions with intention. Stop overanalyzing and trust your gut. Take decisive steps that are in line with your principles and aspirations. Embrace new experiences: Don't let overthinking hold you back. Venture beyond the boundaries of your comfort zone and discover uncharted opportunities.

Nurture connections with supportive individuals who uplift and inspire you. It is important to acknowledge that seeking professional assistance demonstrates strength rather than vulnerability. There will be moments when old patterns resurface. Be kind to yourself, acknowledge the slip, and gently redirect your focus. With consistent practice and self-compassion, you'll strengthen your mental muscle and reclaim control of your thoughts.

As you move forward, remember the impact you can have. Share your journey, inspire others, and help break the stigma surrounding mental health. By empowering others, you empower yourself and create a ripple effect of positive change.

You are not alone. You have the strength, resilience, and resources to overcome overthinking and thrive. Believe in yourself, embrace your journey, and go forth with courage and compassion. The world needs your unique light, unburdened by overthinking. Shine brightly!

Remember, this is just the beginning. Keep exploring, keep growing, and keep reminding yourself: you are worthy, capable, and free.

Bonus Section

This bonus section is a few pages from the official workbook for this book - "Stop Yourself from Overthinking". You can get it from Amazon. It'll help to truly make this book your own and have a chance to practicalize all you've learned.

Chapter 1: The Many Faces of Overthinking

In this chapter we learn about the different spectrums of overthinking and the many faces it can take on human beings. For example, someone may be overthinking, and he might see himself as a strategist, a critic or an analyzer. Another person will see himself as the worrier, the perfectionist, the doubter or the planner. All these are faces of overthinking but the person it's happening to doesn't know what is happening That is why overthinking has become an epidemic.

Again, we have different spectrums like catastrophizing, doubting, rumination, mind-reading, and so on.

Here are some questions that will help you whether you are really overthinking while in the guise of any of the above faces of overthinking.

- Do you ever find yourself trapped in a mental labyrinth, endlessly replaying past conversations, dissecting decisions, and worrying about future possibilities?
- Does your mind become your worst critic, replaying negative scenarios on repeat? Does "analysis paralysis" grip you, preventing action?
- Do you feel drained and anxious after hours of mental rumination?

Use this space below to put down your answers.

My Thoughts

____

____

____

____

____

____

____

Additional Reading and Resources

Books:
- Feeling Good: The New Mood Therapy by David D. Burns: This classic CBT workbook guides you through identifying and challenging negative thought patterns.
- The Mindful Way Through Anxiety by Mark Williams, John Teasdale, Zindel Segal, and Jon Kabat-Zinn: This book teaches mindfulness techniques to manage anxiety and overthinking.
- Quiet: The Power of Introverts in a World That Can't Stop Talking by Susan Cain: This explores the introverted mind and offers strategies for managing overthinking tendencies.
- The Gifts of Imperfection by Brené Brown: This book encourages self-compassion and acceptance as a path to overcoming self-doubt and negative thinking.

Websites and Articles:
- Rethinking Rumination https://journals.sagepub.com/doi/abs/10.1111/j.1745-6924.2008.00088.x
- Anxiety and Depression Association of America (ADAA): https://www.adaa.org/: https://www.adaa.org/

- National Institute of Mental Health (NIMH): https://www.nimh.nih.gov/health/topics/anxiety-disorders: https://www.nimh.nih.gov/health/topics/anxiety-disorders
- The Jed Foundation: https://jedfoundation.org/: https://jedfoundation.org/
- Headspace: https://www.headspace.com/: https://www.headspace.com/
- Calm: https://www.calm.com/: https://www.calm.com/

Podcasts:
- The Happiness Lab with Dr. Laurie Santos: <invalid URL removed>: <invalid URL removed>
- The Mindful Self-Expression Podcast: <invalid URL removed>: <invalid URL removed>
- Therapy for Black Girls: https://therapyforblackgirls.com/podcast/